Stealt[illegible]

Lincoln Lockdown Made Me Do It

Austin Macauley Publishers™
London • Cambridge • New York • Sharjah

About the Author

Photography by Calvin Taylor Lee

Peter Jackson was raised in Ireland and studied Natural Sciences at Trinity College Dublin. In his late teens/early 20s, he hitchhiked extensively around Europe and to/from India. He was briefly a microbiologist before moving to England to join the Royal Air Force as a navigator flying mostly on Victors (air to air refuelling) and Sentry aircraft (the radar/eye in the sky), involved in several of the recent conflicts.

He married Helen Blake in 1973 and is the proud father of Owen, Orla and Niamh. He lives in Lincoln and Javea, Spain.

“This is a delightful collection.

Peter explores many existential issues that face us. He quizzically examines life, age, time, identity, and feelings. As he himself says: he has a degree in curiosity!

He certainly shows it with self-deprecating humour, and appreciation of nature’s beauty and variety, and the complexities of the human situation. He gives no definitive answers to the puzzles of life, but sows tantalising hints of the depths that surround us. This is a collection worth exploring, and re-reading. It has many valuable insights.

I heartily recommend it.”

– Dr Timothy Jackson, Specialist in Public Health Medicine (Retired), Poet

“All of us dealt with the challenges of the pandemic lockdowns in different ways. Peter wisely chose to record his innermost thoughts and feelings in a series of insightful, moving, courageous and often amusing poems. This collection of his works will resonate with all who have the privilege of reading them.”

– Simon Fielding OBE, Chair of Trustees The College of Medicine.

“OMFG !”

– Heather Tebb, hearing ‘Heroes’

Dedication

This book, and any royalties, is dedicated to YMCA, Nomad Trust and the Salvation Army, excellent bodies of people who offer hope, dignity and temporary housing to those in need.

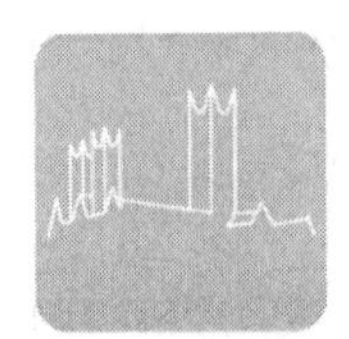

NOMAD

PART OF **YMCA** LINCOLNSHIRE

Acknowledgements

I'd like to say thank you to the people who brought me to today: Helen and our great children Owen, Orla and Niamh for teaching me to love and be loved. Earlier: my father for the foundation of values, sisters Anabella for keeping the drafts out for a troubled youth and Susan for awakening my slack mind, George Warren for his infectious sense of humour, Bea Jackson for being a saint and stormtrooper in "God's Underground", Helen's mother Teresa and her brother Father Jack for welcoming me unconditionally into their family at a time when 'religious' background was heavily stratified in Ireland, my imaginary brothers Michael Warren and Tim Jackson - both exceptional, Bruce Lambert, a constant friend since age 4, Simon Fielding who taught me to dive and laugh louder at myself. All more than I deserve.

Many friends and family kept the wind in my sails. These writings simply would not exist had they not taken the time and trouble to enthuse about and critique my fledgling efforts. Thank you.

Going to the (publishing) market was a new experience. Austin Macauley made it easy for me from first contact with Ishmael Quigley to Matthew Prince answering all my questions several times to everyone who took the phone calls in a bright cheerful manner. Once 'accepted', Ethan Scurrah brought me through the production phase and designed the very fine book cover. I am indebted to his boundless youthful enthusiasm, his flexibility and rapid responses at every stage.

Table of Contents

Friends and Family

Poems B.C. (COVID - 2017)

Foreword

When I am older and more past it than I am now, you will find me walking, talking to myself and chuckling, relishing past highlights such as:

Hitchhiking: Stepping in from the cold into a warm car or truck, welcomed by a complete stranger out of kindness or boredom, conversation my sole currency of gratitude. Back then, childhood, adolescent confusion and independence all took (me) longer, hitchhiking a way of breaking out of and away from my shell. Feeling free to stumble through hazy unformed thoughts, peeking into the lives of others, unfettered by the expectations and constraints of family background, school and college, religious and social boundaries (it was late 60's Ireland after all).

COVID: a similar experience. Stumbling on a secret in plain sight - writing. Writing to understand, to listen for the dormant flow, to find connections and connectedness, to aspire, to share insights and instincts on this journey together from A to B.

Retired now, I acquired the nickname of Stealth in the Royal Air Force, hence StealthWorks. There are many family nicknames layered with years of love and teasing each other, hence Pape Poems. My children mock me when telling a jokey reference, my check whether they had heard and understood when they didn't react with thunderous applause. I have tried to avoid this here.

I'll open with "What has COVID ever done for us ?" and end with "A Lesson Learnt". Everything else is in chronological order mirroring the passing seasons, real-world events, my own experience.

This is my first attempt at writing publicly; if you find the style and content get more confident and stronger you'd probably be right. I often read magazines backwards and this may serve you well here, working backwards from Poem 83. 'Friends & Family' is self-explanatory. Read these kindly as 'slight to moderate' as per the Shipping Forecast may be appropriate.

While friends and family will know me better from reading these, my hope is that others will see their own reflections clearer and more sympathetically.

Peter Jackson / StealthWorks
Lincoln
14 September 2022

1.

"What Has COVID Ever Done for Us ?"

Certain sounds seem much more clear,
the tone and warmth of voices dear,
tendrils of friendship coming down the phone
remind me that tho' solitary, I am not alone.

Time to pause and time to think,
undoubtedly, there's time to drink !
Time to assess what works for me,
become the person I want to be.

Why have I never quite seen trees and flowers ?
Heard the thrill of birdsong in leafy bowers ?
Seen the changing light as seasons go past ?
Everything so beautiful, tho' not meant to last.

Time to pause and watch a star,
we are so much more than we think we are,
but we can not realise this beautiful fact
if every moment of our day with ‘stuff' is packed.

We think we will live forever
and have not yet been proved wrong.
Now is a time which calls for courage.
Now is a time to be strong ...

Apologies to Reg, People's Front of Judea (Life of Brian)

StealthWalks in Lincoln South Common,
Christmas Morning 2020

2.

Nature

Nature does not perform its dance for me.
What am I thinking ? How can it be ?

Is Nature pleased when I notice its charm,
its grace and beauty ? Does it show alarm
when I hurry scurry past, oblivious ?

A big resounding “No” to both,
the sad fact being, tho' I am loathe
to admit:

I am invisible to her.
I do not exist to her.
I am irrelevant to her.

But before I subside into adolescent rage,
I'll pause ,
and turn another page,
to ask a better question.

StealthSees Nature afresh, 27 April 2020

3.

COVID-19

Do we now reconsider our definition of life ?
That a minute dead thing can cause such strife.

Strike enormous fear into our hearts,
the nightly death toll, enough for a start.

Our breathing surface the size of Centre Court
is as nothing if to ICU you are not brought ...
Now !

Or our overzealous foot soldiers of defence,
press the button and whoosh, problems immense.

Rewind, rewind to an earlier day,
when no need to keep this beast at bay,
but sadly not an option for me or for you,
we can only grit our teeth and see it through ...

StealthWorks (Lincoln Lockdown), 10 May 2020

4.

A Sadness

(Tory Leadership announce they are prepared to forego the Northern Ireland Protocol which they had only recently written into law)

How has this Country
become ...
what it is ...
today ?

Why are we surprised
at the lies
that fly
from the mouth of the liar ?

What do words mean,
if the mind is not clean,
the intention not true ?
I leave it to you ...

to decide

StealthWorks *(Lincoln Lockdown), 10 September 2020*

5.

On A Lighter Note

All my life I've wanted to be whole,
like a shape that would fit in a bowl,
but I've learnt since then,
from the teachings of Zen,
Life doesn't always rhyme ...

Almost three score years and eleven,
by this stage I should be in Heaven.
Am I now waiting for
that knock on my door ?
Feck No ! I'll make ninety seven !

(to be confirmed)

We've all turned into Steve Jobs overnight,
for sure, no need to wear anything bright.
Why look the part ?
Or dress up smart ?
Especially when trousers are tight.

StealthWorks, 12 September 2020

6.

If I Was a Tree ...

If I was a tree,
oh please humour me,
I'd stand tall, as tall as the sky.

I'd watch the sunrise
and hear the birds' cries
while you, in your bed, you still lie.

I'd stand fast in the wind
and wait in the rain,
the snow, it would not defeat me.

To know all the birds' names
and watch squirrel games,
a veritable saint from Assisi.

But I am too old
and I so feel the cold,
this would be harder than 26 miles.

But if there's a red scarf round a tree,
it could just possibly be me,
so walk by with a wink and a smile !

StealthWorks, 5 October 2020

7.

The Sentinel

Let us go then, you and I.
You who'll be with me till the day I die.
You who have known me from the very start.
You who knows every working of my head and heart.
You who have heard every word I've said.
A silent presence, always there, at the foot of the bed.

You know full well the man I can be,
which is not the same as the person I see.
Someone who faffs and fails, easily tired,
I turn to you to be inspired.
Help me discover love and light,
help me to heal, help me not to take fright
at the challenge of changing my rutted ways.
A start would be keeping the red wine at bay !

Help me find purpose, help me to choose,
so much of the rest I can happily lose.
I want to be a person my children can admire,
live the values I respect and to which I aspire.
Three score and eleven but my journey's not done,
in fact, in many ways, it's only just begun.
Let us go then, you and I,
walk together on the road, to a brighter sky.

StealthWorks *(Lincoln Lockdown), 17 October 2020*

8.

The Existential Angst of Thomas the Tree

I don't feel quite myself today.
I want to stop it all, go out to play,
tear up my roots and stride out
to the amazement of the passing lout.

Could I learn to frolic and play ?
Like the dogs I see while their owners shout "Stay !"
But to what purpose, what can I do ?
Though I watch life, can I be like you ?

Can I ever escape my "roots ?"
For you, it's as easy as old boots.
What is my purpose, what can I offer ?
If you just say "Logs", I'll sigh and boff yer.

You take what's mine, the "branch" and "roots",
Family Tree metaphors, for when it suits.
But do you really understand my life ?
The digging, the reaching, the continuous strife.

Though the heavens rain on me from on high,
I take my drink in the dark where my roots lie.
I need no calendar to remind me of God's love,
of the sun's journey in the firmament above.

And your breath's waste products, I lap up
to return fresh air for you to sup,
so we are connected, you and me.
Next time you breathe in, please thank me.

StealthWorks, *18 October 2020*

9.

Well there you have it !

Take it from me,
I have a degree
in curiosity.

“That's not much,” you say,
but it brightens my day
and that's what matters to me.

Just look at your hands,
the whorls and the bands,
there's no one who's quite like you.

And your DNA,
just 4 building blocks at play,
a unique blueprint in you they imbue.

So what does it all mean ?
What can we glean ?
from this incredible miraculous fact ?

We should become who we are,
or the Powers that Be from afar
will have completely wasted their time !

StealthWorks, 1 November 2020

10.

For Johnny Fincham Palmist & Wise Man of The East (Norfolk)

Have you ever had your hand read ?
Heard the full A to Z
of the lines and the shape of your hand ?

Have you smelt the black ink
which your hand seems to drink
to show the map of this hidden land ?

Did you not know,
that as you grow,
the Artist inside chips away ?

Your hands show it all,
every climb, every fall,
there's nothing else that you need to say.

What can it all mean,
these forces unseen,
that faithfully depict who you are ?

We are not alone in life,
through the trouble and the strife,
Hallelujah, Hallelujah, Hallelujah !

StealthWorks, 12 November 2020

11.
The Last Leaf

Oh please, don't make me go,
don't make me go with the flow
which saw all of the others depart.

I'm hanging on tight,
out of fear, out of fright,
and I say this with all of my heart.

Why can't I just stay,
forever and a day,
just as it always was ?

Give me reason, any reason,
for death in this season,
and please don't just say "Because".

The wind's coming fast,
I'm not sure I can last,
my grip becomes steadily weaker.

Then with just one more blow,
I – can – feel – myself – let
- go.

Whoosh ....
...
..
.

StealthWorks, 14 November 2020

12.

T(ea) is for Tyrant

You may see her as sweetness and light,
her eyes are so lovely and bright
but her first deed of the day,
if you're weak, look away,
is to Pull Back the Covers and Shout:

"Tea, Tea, Tea !
Tea, Tea for Me !"

Every night as I lay down in bed,
I dread what I know lies ahead,
I have nightmares galore
of her shouts at full bore:

"Tea, Tea, Tea !
Tea, Tea, for Me !"

Does this story end well, do you think ?
She transforms as she takes the first drink,
she's so thoughtful, she's so kind,
no one else quite springs to mind.

So I'll put up with:

"Tea, Tea, Tea !
Tea, Tea, for Me !"

StealthWorks after getting bed tea, 14 November 2020

13.

An Incomplete Poem

The sun rises, but this of course is wrong,
Earth spins backwards, the sun stands still and strong.

So much of life is like this,
our understanding wrong or incomplete.
How do we discover who we are ?
How do we find our feet ?

Do spiders ask these questions
while busy with their web ?
Do large oaks have these doubts
while seasons flow and ebb ?

Separate from Nature, it is hard to know our nature
with our artificial fires and light.
If we could see into our eyes
would we find them dull or bright ?

But our eyes look resolutely outwards,
like guns pointing the wrong way,
so what to do ?
I'm asking you,
or do you too have 'feet of clay' ?

StealthWorks, 29 November 2020

14.

Mirror, Mirror on the Wall

When you look in the mirror, what do you see ?
An older person, who can **that** be ?
“Help ! Help ! Let me out ! Let me out !”
There's been a mistake, I rant and I shout.

I'm a younger, fitter, more vigorous man.
How did I get here ?   What is the plan ?
I remember so clearly all the people I've been,
they still live inside me tho' it seems sight unseen.

When younger I couldn't see beyond your grey hair,
so now that it's my turn, I can't claim it's unfair.

StealthAvoids mirrors, 16 December 2020

15.

Do Trees Cry ...?

Do trees cry as their leaves fall ?
An old oak replied: "No, not at all.
You look on any change with such fright,
not having faith that day follows night."

"The flip side of Autumn is Spring,
they are bound in an eternal ring.
So when you realise this, give a shout,
to breathe in, you must first breath out."

StealthWorks, 16 December 2020

16.
Tea For Me

The Buddhist teacher carefully preparing tea,
poured on, poured on to show that "Me"
and "Mine" leave little space
for Love to grow and show us Grace.

StealthWorks, 16 December 2020

17.

Feeling "Blah"

(An expression coined by Uncle Jeremy)

I feel tired,
so uninspired,
what should I do with my life ?
After I've made tea for my wife.

I feel weary,
my eyes are bleary,
what shall I do today ?
The sky is so very grey.

I feel cross,
just at a loss,
how will I spend the next hour ?
Where, oh where is my power ?

I hardly know I'm alive,
I want to sleep not strive,
I'm fed up,
I give up.

Time ticks patiently on ...

Tick-tock ... tick-tock ... tick-tock ...

Waiting ...

StealthWorks, 18 December 2020

18.

Post Brexit

What will we discuss now that Brexit is done ?
and the era of Trump has almost had its run ?
What will we find to occupy our thoughts ?
Because something will.

How much energy and time do we expend ?
Westminster, the White House, it's all a dead end.
Is there no better way to spend our precious time ?
Walk for miles, read a book or even pen a rhyme.

StealthWorks, 27 December 2020

19.

How To Read a Poem

It seems only fair,
if you want to prepare,
to share my views,
to give some clues,
for what you might do
when your inbox calls to you.

Let's start with *The Cat on the Mat.*
Easy you say, *On the Floor by the Door,*
but why not *On the Table in a Stable*
or *Curled up like a Ball on the Wall* ?
In the realm of the poem it's impossible to fall
if the author prefers levity to gravity.

You don't like Cats you say.
Well there's *The Dog and the Frog*
or this other with a ring,
say, *The Bee who had no Sting.*

Ping! You are cordially invited
to attend this event.
You can sing, you can dance
or sit as in a trance.

You see a poem is an invite
which requires your appetite.
It is for You to complete
or it simply cannot be replete...

StealthWorks, 30 December 2020

20.

2021 ... What Kept You?

Welcome ... Welcome to 2021 !
This is the year we'll have some fun,
(again)
This is the year we'll make COVID run,
(away)
This is the year we'll splash and play.
We'll be able to shout, Hip Hip Hooray !

Give thanks for those things that kept us surviving,
the smiles of strangers, always reviving.
Walking outdoors in spring, autumn and summer,
shrugging off the feeling that life is a "bummer".
Wearing the same clothes day after day,
I'm sure I could give my wardrobes away.
(without noticing)

Realising so many people have had it much worse,
if you're reading this poem, you are lucky, not cursed.
We should try to stay strong
and keep going on ...

Welcome ... Welcome to 2021 !

StealthWorks, 8 January 2021

21.
Murphy Who Lives at No 12

I have a new friend called Murphy,
Murphy is his name.
Every day I go to his house to see if he is game,
to run and play, play and run,
but first, he stops at No 8.
His excitement rises, he strains and pulls,
as we rush through our front gate.

I unleash the hound,
and off he bounds,
scittering along the floor.
"Where - is - She ?   Where - is - She ?"
if he could speak, this would be his roar.

He gallops upstairs,
he can not bear,
not to see Her right away.
He leaps on the bed
and lies down "dead".
This is the best part of his day ...
(& mine)

StealthWalks Murphy, 9 January 2021

22.

Life Without a Tail

If only we had a tail to wag,
to show that we are friends.
How great to have simple signals
to quickly make amends.

But being 'Superior Beings',
we have dispensed with all of this.
So we endlessly make life hard for ourselves,
needing more than a bone for bliss.

How did we lose these simple ways ?
Why are we now so complicated ?
Is this really who we want to be ?
Is this the life that is fated ?

Que No !

We should speak our truth simply,
it'll be difficult until we try.
If it doesn't work out, we'll have done our best,
let our gravestones read this when we die.

StealthWorks, 10 January 2021

23.

Sleep

Can anyone tell me why we need to sleep ?
When your mind recedes and you drop into the deep.
“Actually, Bactually” as Aoife would say,
only “Surface Mind” with “Deeper Mind” still at play.

Who else to mind the plumbing and maintain the heartbeat ?
And all that other stuff between tip of head and feet.
And the dreams, oh the dreams, where do **they** come from ?
That crazy spider web of images mostly forgotten by the dawn.

Who is the Conductor that runs that carousel ?
The spinning thoughts and images endlessly running till the bell,
and who is the Librarian who controls my memory bank ?
Faces, pets and scary dreams, my mind is never blank.

What does it all amount to ?
I'd be wiser if I knew,
but I have my suspicions,
as I'm sure, my friend, do you...

StealthSleeps, 12 January 2021

24.

A Haiku (Get You !)

“In the Long Grass”

(Michael Warren, who gave me encouragement & TS Eliot)

If I could inform,
if I could utter my piece,
what words would I say ?

♫ Teach your Children Well ♫

“Teach your children well.”
Did Neil Young follow these words
when he had young Youngs ?

StealthWorks, 14 January 2021

25.

Stand Tall

If you wobble,
if you fall,
Stand Tall, Stand Tall.

When you feel
Faint of Heart,
Look the Part, Look the Part.

The problem, can you see,
is that deep inside you and me
is a child before the age of 4.
Most cannot see beyond this door.

What happened there is a closed book,
the first chapters missing, how to look
and understand ?
Not possible, No admission.
For this, you don't have our permission.

What we experienced then, we do not know,
love's glow or scar tissue and such to show ?

I used to think someone else was to blame
for my various faults and sense of shame,
but now I see, it's all down to me,
however else could it possibly be ...

StealthStands a little taller, 15 January 2021

26.

Life After Death ?

What do you think about Life after Death ?
That passage that starts when you can't find your breath,
when your heart stops beating, no hope of revival.
What then is your instinct on further survival ?

We've all heard the tales of near-death on the table,
the tunnel of light, silver thread... all fable ?
What if it's true and death's passing through a veil
to a different consciousness, what then will prevail ?

I imagine a rocket launching into deep space,
jettisoning stages one by one when they've run their race.
People of our age already sense how this goes,
I can still see my toes
but that's as far as it...

So do you wait in a queue to meet the Great Maker ?
Who would see straight away if you were only a faker,

or do you stand in front of a mirror

and see

yourself ?

StealthWorks, 15 January 2021

27.

God Speaking,
A Poem for The Faint-Hearted

‘Oh Almighty God, give me a sign, show us a sign.’
Dear God, when I hear this, I want to resign,
talking to myself is bad for a start,
a tell-tale sign that I'm losing heart.

Where on earth is their life lens of wonder ?
Why can't they see ?
Can they not ponder ?

Despite the widespread disease and strife,
can they not see that all of life
is a mystery revealing divine love ?
Instead they cry out to the heavens above.

Be Quiet! That's an order I give from on high,
walk in my garden and you'll see, bye and bye.
There are signs all around you,
I don't know where to begin,
so listen to Nature and try not to give in.

If you really want to know Me,
look into the eyes of a child.
When you grasp that, you can forget the rest,
so for My sake, smile and just do your best ...

StealthWorks, 15 January 2021

28.

Musing Murphologically, A Ditty of No Consequence

Ringggggggggggg !!

Let - Me - In ! Let - Me - In !
and let the fun begin.
Chase me, Chase me quickly upstairs,
you won't catch me, not even a hair,
bound onto the bed...
What's that under the 'spread ?
Burrow, Burrow, Burrow, Burrow ...

I sneak up on the dog,
who's now lying like a log,
head on my pillow, he knows
how the other half lives, it shows.
I attack the hound
but he escapes with one bound,
and lies on my chest licking my face,
I laugh hysterically, losing the race ...

Can we go for that walk now... ?

StealthWalks, 18 January 2021

29.

"If One is a Greyhound, Why Try to Look Like a Pekinese ?"

For Mary E - A Greyhound's View

I wish I had a nobler head,
I so dislike the way I'm bred.
Imagine lustrous wavy hair,
my own just drives me to despair.
My dreams are full of fires and laps,
my life spent bolting out of traps.

You see I'm raised purely and solely for speed,
not for spoiling and pampering like your Pekinese.
No one loves me for who I am,
my exercise is functional - the training plan.
No one plays with me, say Hide and Seek,
and God help me when I grow weak ...

Just ask Santa's Little Helper ...

StealthWorks, 20 January 2021

30.

Last Wednesday

(Amanda Gorman - 20 January 2021)

Did you hear it ? What was that sound ?
It was long-lost Purpose found.
A shout from her heart,
it gave me quite a start !
A tigress dressed in yellow,
Man ! Did she ever bellow !

We have been asleep for so very long,
there should be shame that the one who is strong
is a young black woman of twenty-two,
"Elders and Betters" ? Puh ! I leave it to you ...

A clarion call, a flag unfurled,
this is the time for this suffering world
to heal.

The Call Up is for all
to do something, no matter how small,
to draw your line in the sand,
by no one else to be defined,
to overcome weakness and fight with your might,
now look in your heart, doesn't this feel right ?

StealthWorks better on inspiring Inauguration Days,
25 January 2021

31.
More Than We Deserve

Every day the sun rises higher in the sky,
as we in lockdown live our lives on standby.
Soon there will be a glorious spring,
buds will flower again, birds will sing.
Nature moves gracefully in its own measured pace.
This is how it is... this never was a race.

The Silent Conductor lightly rearranges,
with the catalyst of strength and length of light,
to bring about continual changes,
days now grey will soon once more be bright.

"Barren" branches will soon flower again,
give thanks for this cycle of life... Amen.

StealthWorks better when January is done, 31 January 2021

32.

Early February ...

First the yellow Aconites,
“that's Buttercups, no need for fright.”
The bright bed of Yellow, a clarion call,
better times ahead for one, for all.

Next the Snowdrops purest White,
modest heads drooping away from light.
Symbolising Hope in the coming season,
as a purpose in life, no better reason.

Now Crocuses push up through soggy ground,
nature is so varied, haven't you found ?
Their subtle colours; a joy to behold.
Winter retreats, this is better than gold ...

StealthWorks better as days lengthen, 05 February 2021

33.

A Cat Never Blinks First ...

In ancient times cats were worshipped as gods;
they have not forgotten this.

You can't bring your cat for a walk,
at this, they most definitely balk,
and your cat won't chase after a stick
"Who Me ?''
"Are you mad ?"
"Am I thick ?"

"What you want is a daft servile mutt
and I am most certainly not of that cut.
Long ago I was of Royal Ascendancy,
so there can be no question of dependency,
unless on your part ...

When I sit, sphinxlike, at the window,
I relive the past glories of my clan.
My kind has roamed the earth,
almost since time began.

You may home me but don't own me.
However else could it be ?
I accept your tithes of food for "your treasure"
and usually other neighbours' for good measure ..."

StealthRemembers furry feline friendship, 8 March 2021

34.

A Kind of Magic

Now then... Each year, about this time,
we are witnesses to a process quite sublime.
Winter's x-rays of stark bare trees
will transform by magic in front of you and me.

No sudden flourish of cape revealing all,
but day by day changes, each quite small,
all rushing slowly to a majestic display.
Don't believe me ? - You just wait till May ...

What shocks the arboreal corpse to life ?
After long winter months of cold, rain, strife,
buds swelling, leaves starting to appear,
soon the crescendo of blossom we hold so dear.

The Crown Princes Xylem and Phloem reinstated
as days lengthen, they work unabated.
Miracles around us which we take for granted,
the magic of light shining on a life enchanted ...

StealthWorks, 14 March 2021

35.

Exponential

This word used to live in dark drawers,
brought blinking to light and low roar
of apathy.
Chalk scratching to the drone
of the teacher,
back to class,
all alone.

Now ...
Now we understand,
the staircase graph showing band
of infections, worse, of death,
the tragic fight for one's very own breath.

We assume that we are Masters of the Universe,
but we realise now this is false and perverse.
COVID-19, a part of Nature after all,
reminds us to respect Her lest we continue to fall...

StealthWorks, 06 April 2021

36.

The Black Spot (Treasure Island)

I wander and wonder,
what else can one do ?
Nature has so much to offer,
day by day, for me, for you.

Life resurrects before our eyes,
from "dead" trees, fresh buds appear.
Though we have seen this times before,
in this time of COVID, it feels so dear.

And the new-found flowers
appearing from dark solid earth,
"Reaching Up, Pushing Out,"
with this sturdy mantra, we see their birth.

But the face in the mirror,
how will it answer this call ?
The apple eaten cannot be returned.
Do we learn or continue to fall ?

StealthWorks, 6 April 2021

37.

An Irish Airman Forsees His Birthday

(apologies to W B Yeats)

“All days are special, but some are more special than others,”
as Animal Farm's Napoleon never said.
My Special Day starts very strongly,
opening cards & presents beside Helen in bed.

It is lovely to be reminded you are loved,
even Facebook does good on this Day,
lighting up the World Wide Web of friendship,
keeping life's trivial worries at bay.

So, glass in hand, I'll stand up and salute you
and thank you for all your kindly acts;
I would not be who I am without you,
love is a mighty power and that's a fact !

Stealth's Special Day, 26 April 2021

38.

Fanfare !!!

(A fan writes of Marcus Aurelius)

The lessons learnt from bygone years
have not changed.
So, to avoid more tears,
we must pay attention to what you wrote at night,
fortunately translated, I'm not **that** bright ...

You knew that what will be, will be,
that's still the same for you and me.
We don't have your wars or nations to rule,
but we still rail against fate, aren't we the fool ?

Can we slow the clock, reverse our age ?
Looking back as we do, rewrite the page ?
Good luck with all that; you may have found a way,
I'll just do what I can and enjoy today ...

StealthQueues at Centro de Salud, Javea
(a small glimpse of eternity)
28 June 2021

39.

Bracebridge Quarantine Blues

Ten days may not seem a lot,
but I mourn my “loss”, not what I've got.
Sighing forlornly through windows like Alcatraz,
people walked by dogs, kids skipping, all that jazz ...

Of course, we are not all alone,
chats to friends and family on the telephone,
our lovely neighbours helping in every way,
which brightens, lightens our 'lonely' day.

The Stoic in me watches on,
he waits patiently for me to see beyond
my temporary confinement;
I cannot walk in woods today,
but I can use this time to sit, think, even pray,
that I can learn that “All Things Pass”,
not live out my days as an ass !

StealthWorks even in quarantine, 9 July 2021

40.

How Long Have We Got ?

In the kitchen surrounded by packets and tins,
many “Out of Date”, past their “Best Before”.
Who makes these arbitrary decisions ?

Some people define themselves by physical prowess,
or by their careers, so when these pass ...
If fortunate, grandchildren are a gift of mostly delight
to reinvigorate the flagging senses.

But we should be wary of being defined by others,
better to maintain or find our own enthusiasms,
go into the darkroom and watch the silver outline take shape ...

After all,
how long have we got ?

StealthSteps out of line from rhyme, 10 July 2021

41.

The Weight of Words

I am not afraid to plagiarise
the words and truths of others.
There is no “missing link”,
no short cut,
only insights glimpsed and forgotten
many times.
Pearls discovered, then released
for the next intrepid diver.

It used to annoy me,
people quoting “my” lines as their own
but there is no copyright for casual utterance.
Now I smile,
“Imitation the greatest flattery” after all !

So when you speak
and answer one of my troubling questions,
we are both victorious,
both Giver and Receiver,
both enhanced in the “Aha!” moment,
the veil lifted,
light briefly streaming in.

StealthWorks even on 12 July 2021

42.

Confessional

(For Rebecca, "Cutting It", Bracebridge Heath)

The woman sits down,
tightlipped.
Her thin smile
does not reach her weary eyes.
Eyes which are unfocused,
scanning other horizons.

The process starts,
warm water relaxing tight nerves.
She settles down to the
private personal pampering.
This, her oasis
from the constancy of her daily life alone.

These days,
little point talking about holidays,
as almost a cruelty,
her plans suspended.

"How are you coping ?"

The woman talks,
baring herself in her unhappiness.
Her doctor, though kind,
has not the time,
can only offer advice and pills,
neither needed nor wanted,
and the Church is no longer a refuge.

But here,
here in this chair,
she can unburden herself,
speak out all her fears and frustrations,
without interruption.
And spoken from her lips,
she sees things in proportion.

There is no need for absolution
nor token penance,
neither has she sinned,
just found herself unequal
to the miasma of fearful uncertainty
as so many others ...

She rises, seemingly taller,
adjusts her hair approvingly,
tips generously, smiles broadly,
walks out renewed.

StealthWorks, 15 July 2021

43.

The Constant Gardener

My mother lived to garden,
cooing to her “treasures” daily,
dead-heading her “meditation”.

Imagine
if we could do the same
for ourselves,
removing dead buds,
culling the waste
for future growth.

Where to start ?

He procrastinates,
Snip,
Prevaricates,
Snip, snip,
drinks liberally,
Snip, Snip (a bit tough this one) ...

I could go on ...
But to what point ?
We are part of Nature,
but not that part.
Our culling and cropping
is internal,
of our own volition.

Now,
where to start ... ?

StealthSnips, 17 July 2021

44.
Waking

Waking up is important
when you consider the alternatives.
That given,
how you wake up
can define your day, week, life.
So if you awake naturally bright,
optimistic, purposeful,
you are lucky.

But if your mind is recalcitrant,
loathe to leave the dense dream darkness,
all energy spent in nighttime skirmishes,
you wake up all “akilter”,
forced to lean forward to gain momentum,
not lie back into the deadly warm comfort.

In times past,
Life being a struggle was not big news,
quite the opposite.
Youths were set acts of huge courage
before being accepted as young men.
But the days of certainty in roles or authority
are long past.
Each now must find their way.

But the human mind and spirit have not changed.
And still no Instruction Manual after all this time !
At school, we learn Algebra and how the body functions,
though not how our mind works.
How it creates a personal sense of reality,

both a shield to protect and a set of filters,
colouring or darkening the light and life around us.
The foundation stones laid in the "lost" years,
which we can neither change nor remember.

In the Jewish faith, the day starts at sunset,
prayers striking a light in the darkness to come.
Restful regeneration for the daybreak ahead,
not surrendering to listless slumber.

We can also learn from the biblical past,
David soothing King Saul with his music.
We cannot slay our demons,
but we can
live with them,
and in so doing,
find our strength.

StealthWorks, 30 July 2021

45.

Recent History

We have lived through history,
and are now part of it.
“Where were you when JFK died ?”
Newer landmarks, Diana's death or 9/11.

Morse Code then Radio then TV changing us forever,
bringing the lives of others into our homes,
as if they lived and breathed next door.
We, ghostlike on the fringes, watching avidly,
never thinking to look away.

“Distracted from distraction by distraction.”
This written before the age of television,
that Trojan horse eagerly wheeled into our homes,
where it has both grown and multiplied,
spawning other screens which we can carry with us,
so that we are never alone.

We have lived through history,
the flowering of individuality,
as if it had never before existed.
The youthful drive for self-expression,
which saw what it had made and was pleased,
erasing the memory of previous creations,
severing the links with the past,
ignorant of the consequences.

We have witnessed the fall of Rome,
and watched the statues topple,
pulled down by the rabid thirst
for freedom from authority.

The horizon now featureless,
no one to look up to,
our eyes lazily drawn to the artful imposter,
our minds awash with images and sounds,
the tide coming ever quicker and louder,
from the leisurely 45 waves a minute of my youth,
to the frantic 78 waves a second of now,
our natural impulses drowned out
by the clamour of other lives.

The ghosts of Huxley and Orwell must
scratch their heads in puzzled disbelief.

What have we done ?

StealthWorks, 31 July 2021

46.

Blank Page

I wake up to a blank page,
every day a gleaming question mark,
a new journey if I choose.

But the earlier pages and chapters take over,
“He likes this breakfast, that coffee,
a snack at midday,
and 6 o’clock ?
That's time for a well-earned drink, don't you agree ?”

No harm in any of these,
no need to reinvent fire, rework the wheel,
tying shoelaces, not the challenge it once was.
But our mind's desire to catalogue and automate
all our activities and impulses
is something to be wary of,
or the thrill of the blank page,
the open road, will be lost,
and the risk not taken will re-echo
to haunt me.

StealthWatches his habits warily, 1 August 2021

47.

An Irish Airman Foresees the Coming of Autumn

There's a shaggy dog outside my window.
Well not exactly, but it looks like one,
its branches lushly laden with leaves
weaving and waving in the breeze,
like a dog selling paint.

Soon the narrative will change,
as sunlight grows shorter, weaker.
The leaves once so full and strong
will feel more faded and brittle,
no longer scoffing at the wind,
now holding on with weakening strength,
knowing each gust might presage their fall.

We are not rooted in Nature as my tree is,
so do not feel the passing of the seasons
with the same stoic acceptance.
Generations before enjoyed Nature's blossom and Fall,
as will generations to come,
unaware of Time's steady passage,
as we have been.

StealthLooks ahead to Autumn, 15 August 2021

48.

Things Unseen

Insides of my ears,
bald patch lurking
revealed only in barbers' mirrors
and unflattering photographs.

My backside
and all named "back".
The realm below the skin,
rivers of blood and other.
The vat-like stomach,
coiled intestine,
managed by alchemists.
Now what to do with chips and beer ?
that's "bricks without straw" for you.
And those clever clogs,
the hormonal gang.

My expressions, gestures,
mostly unconscious, reflex,
an open book to others.

Excited by ideas,
sudden flash of sunlight,
the windows to the soul
ajar, curtains flapping,
emitting light from deep within.

That deep within.

Good God, I do not know myself at all.
But you do.

StealthWorks on despite seeing little of himself, 23 August 2021

49.

Part Of Me

There is a part of me
needing neither bread nor wine,
whose presence is felt
only in stillness.

No need to startle the birds,
feet rustling fallen leaves
to approach him,
he is there.

I meet him knowing
that he, the silent watcher,
watches me,
and also, through me.

He teaches me,
in words, I can not
and would not describe,
so please do not ask.

He does not leave me,
tho' I leave him,
like a careless lover,
neither is there any reproach
upon my return,
merely a knowing smile.

Each day,
the board reset,
for me to play, hone my skill,
frequently to walk away,
the pieces strewn in falling rain
like the petulant child I can be.

He appears to be alone,
but that is my vision,
not his.

StealthSenses something more, 24 August 2021

50.

Situs Inversus

For what it's worth,
neither did I.

My friend Brian,
is one in 10,000,
his internal organs,
a mirror image of yours.

We may all look alike,
but not be similar
in so many ways.

My friend, Murphy,
stops to chew grass and weeds,
he knows his needs.

This is one trick we've lost,
have scarcely the wit
to pause when full,
elusive pleasure unsated.

Moving on,
stay with me if you will,
while I crane my head to search
the air I need to breath.

StealthWrites remembering his friend Brian from Gata Residencial, 24 August 2021

51.

Post-Olympic Blues

If you are alive,
age will weary you.

No wish to pole vault,
cavort on gym horse,
or jump hurdles,
life sets enough of these.

Desire to run a marathon long past,
no need to size up other runners,
but our mettle still waits for the shot ...

The course changes with time,
less physical more mental,
and dare I say it, spiritual.

Dare ! Dare !
No route to best without daring,
there are still chasms to climb,
without security of carefully raked sand.

This is a meal for one,
each must choose their own,
alone in my effort
to inhabit my initials,
PB before Personal Best known,
the challenge from my father
accepted.

StealthWorks, 26 August 2021

52.
Night

He is awake,
anticipates then feels
the hand reaching over,
blindly dunking
like a fairground 'digger'.
Ah, he is there.

For one so strong
this is strange,
but no different
to his nighttime terrors,
panting down blind alleys,
chased by phantom bullies
intent on doing harm,
his involuntary cry for help
quickly reassured.

Love takes many forms.

StealthWorks, 28 August 2021

53.

Autumn Tiptoeing Past My Window

The branches sway and wave,
almost a "So be it" farewell,
the leaves floating, falling, twirling,
their last dance.

There is another call,
young adults leaving bedrooms
they have grown up in,
their childhood ebbing away,
leaving a hollow ache
which is hard to fill.

StealthRemembers, 10 September 2021

54.

Happy Birthday Peter Pan

Happy Birthday Peter Pan,
once a boy, you're now a man,
no doubt working on your wedding plan
with your beloved Wendy.

Before, you led the Lost Boys,
life so full of fun and toys,
skipping deftly round "old" Hook's ploys,
always dancing on your feet.

But seeing Wendy through the glass,
you felt a void that would not pass,
till your shadow sown by Darling lass
to make you whole again.

So for us, what does this story hold ?
If we are to grow, we must be bold,
accept the dark, let it unfold
its secrets to our soul.

StealthWrites from Casa Bosque, 6 October 2021

55.

An Early Stroll

I have not read the book,
but today I walk
on Chesil Beach.

Rising early, my mind awash with dreams,
formless, shape-changing, squirming black eels,
their outlines growing fainter with each step,
till all washed away forever.

I am alone,
the night fisherman in their shelters,
their lines now slack,
unreal to me.

The sea stretches to infinity,
I could walk in a few yards,
swim as long as I wanted,
the horizon would remain untroubled.

I think I am acting with intent,
the mission of my walk after all,
but it slowly dawns that
my breath will rise and fall,
soundlessly like these quiet waves,
my body will go about its business,
not needing my attention.

Am I a speck in the universe,
one of 8 billion, dying and being born as I walk ?
Or am I the custodian of something of value,
where I can hone my senses, martial-like,
sit in silence and be at one with this foreign body ?
Both.

The sun now “rises”,
light grows brighter, stronger, warmer.
A lone seagull lazily wheels above me,
not really hungry, but just in case ...
Everything is changing,
as the waves in timeless patience wash in ...

StealthWalks on Chesil Beach, 17 April 2022

56.

Waking Badly

Don't talk to me,
I am not here yet,
I am not ready,
have not collected myself,
scattered by sleep.

Woken by well-meaning alarm,
any intention from last night long forgotten,
I want to sleep on, if possible forever,
so that I don't have to confront myself,
so that I no longer feel like a discarded puppet,
wooden legs akimbo, strings slackly jumbled.

No point in counting blessings as a mantra,
tried so many times before, always insufficient.

When young, I was the plaything of nightmares,
dreaded night, knowing what awaited,
my spirit disappearing, sinking deeper and deeper.

Once I 'woke' to a deadly spider nesting,
covering my entire crown with sleeky browness,
malevolently resting.
This day, some memory of pluck remained;
I slowly raised my hand to lift a spider limb,
this small act of defiance, this David moment,
calmly confronting the evil that tormented me.
Poof ! Gone.
A real victory in my days of subjugation.

Why does my mind do this to me ?
Why does it create this constant fear and uncertainty
that curls the faint photograph like a flame ?
Why do I allow the feeling that I am not real
but that this craven abject terror is ?

Life is so strange.
I have a choice:

If I do not live my life with some purpose, to some end,
I will be my mind's plaything till the end of my days.
So tomorrow I will wake to the smell and sound
of white lines being laid down, the court prepared.

I am ready.
You can talk to me now.

StealthWakes badly, 15 May 2022

57.

Dorian of Wilde Fame

The picture in the attic smirked,
self-satisfied with the memory
of the flailing failing man below,
the subject of his portrait.

Oh, what joy to be the true image
of the conflicted soul below.
Life is made of small victories
or, the picture mused, many small retreats,
compromises, half-truths, boasts, deceptions.
There is only one way to be truthful, many not to be.

What delicious fun to be the snake on his board,
to see the good intention quickly quenched,
the idealistic urge presaging the rumble-tumble descent.
In the card game of life, winner takes all !

But just when about to 'raise his arms' in victory,
his subject took a final desperate throw,
burst open the door, throwing monstrous light upon the canvas,
and tho' humbled, stumbled with it down below.

His weaknesses displayed, his mistakes apparent,
those who had judged him became strangely silent,
nudged by memories of the image of their lesser selves.

StealthWorks in and out of the attic, 28 April 2022

58.

The Yellow Brick Road

I am a searcher...
normally, for my car keys.
This furtive hunting,
drawers ransacked many times,
demonstrates a simple fact.
If it is not there,
you will not find it there.

Often I find myself
looking for other things in the wrong drawer,
always tempted to take the shorter, easier path,
which invariably does not lead to the goal.
Especially when it comes to yourself,
you must look in the right place.

Not so long ago,
this was not an issue.
Teachers and police were marshals of the external,
doctors for the physical body,
priests and clergy wore the cloth as God's messengers,
and their flock in the main did not question them,
decent people, happy for those chosen to guide them.

But the statues of authority have crumbled,
and we now feel we are on our own.

My mother used to joke that our generation
thought that it had invented sex.
The trail of bread crumbs seems harder to find in
the forest,
but there have always been searchers to leave clues,
tho' we must be careful to be our own broker,
not entrust others to define who we are.

StealthWorks better when his car keys are returned, 28 April 2022

59.

Happy Birthday Ed

30,000 days he proudly proclaimed.

Is it any wonder we wake up tired,
powering up so many memories,
carrying so many stages, events, secrets,
like a weary gastropod with its encrusted shell ?
Each of us, a microcosm of evolution,
of Life unfolding.

How the parameters change !
Described first in days, weeks, months,
by proud parents,
each year a giant's stride when young,
then "I'm 12th grade",
mystifying to older folk.

Things start to speed up
as we fully enter adulthood.
Before long, Time canters off,
a force we no longer control.
Our T-shirt mantra,
“been there, done that,”
silent witness to this uncoupling,
the discarded ratchet dust-covered.

The cliff edge coming into view,
what to do, oh what to do ?
We may pray for immortality or extra time
(to be wasted in a similar fashion)
Life's cul-de-sac, the net ever tightening ...

Rewind ? Only in memories ...
Fast Forward ? This now faint from overuse ...
My Stop will come when the Grand Designer deems fit,
my clock for completion of the inner contract wound down,
whether my tasks have been completed or not,
"Pens down, the examination is over."

But Pause, what does this one do ?
Pause to see the rising dust in the light beam,
hear the children play, see the laughter in their eyes,
feel the warm breath, the damp muzzle,
time returning, time shared, time, time ...

StealthWorks better in time, 7 May 2022

60.

Punctuation

If I were punctuation,
I'd want to be a Question Mark,
Comma, possibly a Semi-Colon,
but **never** an Explanation Mark !!
or a Full Stop.

In life, nothing stops.
We carry on,
both in our living
and in our dying,
as our 'soul' journeys on.

Even then our body goes on,
now breaking down, returning
its elements to nature,
the library book returned.

StealthWorks, 21 May 2022

61.

Life Is So Unfair

The unfairness of depression
is that we feel nothing.
So resolute in avoiding pain,
our clever mind flicks the switch
that connects us to any feeling.

There are drugs that help
numb the pain,
but I want to fight this
on my own.

Alone, arrogant
in the faith that I can win
a battle fought since age 10.

So Colonel, what is the strategy ?
"Feelings are the key,
so all will get their visa,
accept pain, anger, frustration.
Stop being so bloody reasonable !"

We are all travellers
on The Yellow Brick Road.
The way will not be won
by wishful thinking or sharp wit.

Feeling may be just "feeling",
but it is part of what makes us whole.

StealthWorks on, feeling his way, 22 May 2022

62.

Eclipse

The void awaits,
it has not left,
but then, why would it ?

I cannot remember
the comfort of sleep.
My nights are sleep full,
but do not bring respite,
do not bring clarity,
the mud is still suspended,
has not sunk to the bottom.

Sitting in silence helps,
of course,
but too often the pause
is an excuse for my mind
to chunter on,
this and that,
to and fro,
without purpose.

The words of Invictus,
given to me by my father,
a faint rallying cry.
If only I could dream this
so that I wouldn't have to wake up
draped in a white flag.

What helps?
Action,
tho' with handbrake on, gears stiff,
starting seldom easy,
to prove to myself
I can enhance some corner
of the chaos in my world.
Writing helps
order the ant-like thoughts,
pick up the faint scent.

What doesn't help ?
That would fill a book
with grubby pages, read so much.
iPhone, so named
to show the phone and I are one,
slicing and dicing my attention.
Being passive in company
increases my despair.
Alcohol, a declared weakness;
I refuse medication,
then dampen my sorrows
in other ways.

The challenge is here
brushing my cheek.
I can look away if I choose
but will never respect myself
until I accept the silken glove.

I walk
amongst others' gloves,
and tho' I can encourage,

theirs are not my fight,
nor can I allow others,
to take my place.

I have resisted pain forever,
tho' with submission,
never having the courage to raise my head
or even my hand to ask for help
when others had charge of me.

Now I have charge of me.
I will look up onto the skies
from whence cometh my help,
but my eyes do not yet see this,
my ears do not yet hear them,
tho' I know that they are close.

I continue.
This is a test
I have chosen.

StealthWorks on, despite, 24 May 2022

63.

I am a Superficial Person

By which I mean
see only skin deep,
the surface of everything,
as does everyone.

We do not realise what it means
to have only our guesswork,
to never know for sure
what the other is thinking, feeling.
We should have the default
that others are thinking
something we are not.

Worse still, we only see what is Now,
never what was Then.
Entranced by the beauty of youth,
we fail to see the shadow of yesterday,
the first blushes, early endeavours.
Our sight blinded by what is Now,
our imagination silent about what was Then,
to our own cost and loss.

The flower unwatered withers,
as does the person unnoticed;
we do not all have the power
to survive personal drought.
We create and sustain
ourselves and each other.
Let us not fail.

We can ask,
but to be truthful,
people do not always know
what they are feeling,
as they live on the surface as we do,
do not always have the wherewithal
to plumb the depths
of their being.

This is not easy,
nor constant,
the tides change,
moon rises,
we are so many aspects,
both conscious and unconscious.

It may not be given
that we understand,
but we can try.

StealthWorks, 25 May 2022

64.

Stagecraft

What continually surprises me
is your agenda, your thoughts,
your experience of you.

We may think
we share the same stage,
not necessarily.
You are you,
I am I.
How can we forget this ?

Our senses feed our mind
which then creates a picture,
makes "sense" of it all,
guided by whims, moods, feelings,
undercurrents from a source we know not.

Each of us are only stage props
to other people,
to be moved round,
seen in this or that light
depending on their Stage Director.

Oh, you may be Juliet to his Romeo,
feel as one beating heart,
but your stages can and will diverge,
mishaps occur ...

So are we marooned,
castaways on our own islands ?
We are born naked and alone,
and our ending is similar.
But all is not bleak,
we can explore our parts,
learn our lines well,
perform for our own and others' joy,
prompt when needed,
curtsey and depart.
Satisfied.

StealthWorks on and off stage, 26 May 2022

65.

Sometimes the Day Comes all at Once

Waking, empty,
energy gauge on emergency,
the promised top-up gone awry,
hose disconnected or more truthfully never engaged,
the myth of night-time regeneration laid bare.

In truth,
there is more than one lane of traffic,
tho' mind and body are intertwined,
they pulse to separate rhythms.
The body, a living miracle
of countless cells and functions,
fluids, moving parts,
an Engineer's dream.
It lives second by second,
busy with the unseen routine of life,
monitoring itself constantly,
the Inner Policeman directing traffic
to keep it all running smoothly.

Mind, a large part of this, but something else.
That mysterious sense of self
Laid down in early forgotten years,
so rugged in some, so vulnerable in others.
Mind follows its own pathways,
its energy comes from other sources,
less tangible forces apply here.

Now we're in the realms of simple satisfaction
of tasks met, even if only making your bed.
Enthusiasm, recognising the people and pursuits
that invigorate you.
Purpose, the embers within that make all things possible.

Mind, the inner voice of our memory,
reciting the litany of past failures, surrenders,
sins of omission and commission
like a dripping tap.
We must find the staircase
and break down the door
to our projection room,
stop the madly spinning reel,
reset the film ...

There is a spark within us
which only we can reignite.
For many, this is not an issue,
but we must play the hand we're dealt.
We must control that runaway horse within us
and reclaim our power.

StealthWakes poorly, 22 June 2022

66.

The Miracle of Me

I could write
the Miracle of You,
but tho' you are beside me,
your chest rising and falling with your breath,
I cannot feel this,
cannot feel your feet on the ground,
your back against the chair.
I cannot feel your sadness
nor sense your random thoughts.

Oh, I know the steely eye,
when hard words are about to fall,
the laughing eyes when we spark
memories of young pups, dogs or children,
but this is not the same
as being you, being inside you.

I can only be me,
can only feel me,
can only select from the palette available,
whether I want to be happy or miserable.
It's a lifetime skill,
one I am still learning, often forget,
that the shaft of light can balance,
can conquer the bitter taste of defeat.

We are not superhuman,
merely human.
We rise and fall daily,
but I am better when I realise
the miracle of me.

StealthWorks, 23 June 2022

67.

For Bobby

He passed in his sleep.
Where has he gone ?
Leaving me only my memories
and out of date bank statements.

I am happy for you,
you who passed without pain,
who never knew the infirmities of old age,
or made compromises for diminished health.
Going out on your own terms,
how very Bobby.

There is no balm for the shock
but some relief that the memories are untarnished,
not ravaged by age, illness, brain fog.
He died as he was.
A warrior's death.

Squadron Leader Bobby Anderson, Buccaneer (including last tour of Ark Royal) & Tornado GR1 Navigator.
Mourned by Jilly, Jack, Victoria, Watson, many friends,
29 July 2022

68.

Who Are You ?

You go by a name
but who are You ?
Your surname given by your father,
from his father, his father before,
or even your husband,
all fine men no doubt.
But who are You ?

Your first name, how chosen ?
From a beloved aunt ?
A character in a book ?
The sound of the name ?

Often the name you go by has changed,
Lilibet to her family,
or the name can be perfect,
Joy, if that is your nature.

To others, you are known differently,
in numbers & letters to NHS and Passport officials.
You are defined, filed away.

In some faiths, names are surrendered,
your personal life now subsumed in your path to service,
or names of Prophets and Teachers are given,
hoping this will be a shield and a banner
in your life to come.

Even divinities have names
tho' sometimes to utter them is blasphemy.

I know you by your name,
as you know me by mine,
but I try to remember
this is not who you are,
merely the dried skin of a stage
you once might have been.

You can be everything and anything,
I will call you by your "name"
but do it carefully ...

StealthReflects on names, *1 August 2022*

69.

How Do You Feel ?

How I hate this question,
tho' I use it often myself.
The intention well meant, sincere concern,
but the question always too big
for the casual encounter.

The friendly smile, genuine pleasure,
but the words come like a cunning arrow,
weaving round my defences,
finding chinks in my armour,
searching soft unguarded flesh.

Normally, the reflex answer,
"Oh, fine," not wishing to burden the other
or reveal myself.
The accretion of small disappointments & failures
themselves not easy to describe.
Where, oh, where to start ?

We have such faith in language,
its precision of meaning,
and see it as a magic tool for all events,
a hieroglyphic miracle.
It isn't.
Feelings are not objects,
"cat" may describe a cat
but "sorrow" does not begin to define sorrow
"grief", grief and so on...

So I'll answer in metaphor,
I feel like an abandoned train in a siding,
the driver's on strike,
dust is settling on the faux leather,
axle grease congealing,
it'll be slow to start ...

"And how do you feel ?"

StealthWorks on better greetings, 7 August 2022

70.
The Session

Follow my voice ...

Relax your body,
feet lightly on the ground,
bottom nestling in the chair.
Aware of skin surfaces,
arms & hands on your thighs,
thighs on the seat
and, pun intended, soul touching ground.

Moving to a state of silent standby,
aware of the body.
Blood is flowing both to the tips of your toes
and to the crown of your cranium,
returning to heart and lungs,
pumped up the vertical cliffs of your legs.
We think of astronauts, their cumbersome suits,
easy to imagine ourselves as also surviving in an alien world,
our life support system so magical and efficient,
a lifetime guarantee from first to last gasp.

Feel the space within you,
follow your breath in & out, in & out,
like gentle waves lapping on the shore,
your busy mind like a distant radio,
its channel dial blown by the careless wind
from last night's argument to a job undone,
shopping list, birthday looming.

This noisy neighbour can be annoying to be sure
but your inner voice is something to cherish.
We cannot control that which comes from deep
within
but it is wise to gently hold the reins.

StealthHolds onto the saddle, 10 August 2022

71.

Regrets

♫ Regrets, I've had a few
but then again, too ... ♫
No, actually,
quite a few.

A regret of time wasted,
which is a shame really
as I'm now rather good at it.

Conversations not had,
the interesting lives of people now past,
stories heard,
listening careless for the retelling,
details now lost forever.

Advice not taken,
"If only you'd smile more"
still haunts me.
Just don't ask me to smile
for photos.

The extra mile not taken
as not "ready",
the conditions not yet right.

But the one that counts,
not knowing how I felt
when I didn't feel right,
not saying how I felt
and the one time I did,
"Growing pains ..."

Would I be anyone else ?
No offence, but no.
Would I do it all again ?
Tricky one that ...
could go either way ...
Several of life's potholes
somehow avoided.

Do I regret having regrets ?
No.

StealthLives with his regrets, 18 August 2022

72.

My Staff

I am three score and thirteen,
past the biblical age.
What can I be now ?
What do I want ?
What can I inhabit ?

I will plant my staff in the earth
and state that I will,
declare that I can,
intend that I will be
something I have not yet been.

Dreams are made with intentions.
Who we are starts
with who we want to be,
not always easy,
but hey,
"If you want an easy life,
you should have joined the Air Force."
(Crimson Tide)

StealthWorks on unresolved issues, 19 August 2022

73.

Heroes

My sisters were war babies.
We grew up in the shadow of strength and valour,
men and women who had greatness thrust upon them
by the troubled times they had lived through,
becoming something greater than themselves
which they carried with dignity ever afterwards.

Like me, television was a small child,
quiet, barely noticed in the corner,
but films showed tales of courage and character,
heroes to look up to.
Books, "Famous Five", "Secret Seven"
entranced me with tales of running free,
saving the day,
before the clammy hand of "stranger danger."

Much has been taken down since then,
the implicit authority of any adult or body
long forgotten ...

And in its place ...
What ?
People famous for being famous,
celebrity culture
rewarded beyond belief.

"What is your Super Power ?"
replaces "Who is your hero ?"
Make believe and special effects the order of the day.
If our children have no one to look up to,
nothing of value to aspire to,
how can they grow ?

We'll find out ...

StealthWatches with concern, 22 August 2022

74.

"The North Wind Made the Vikings"

Or,
"Calm waters never forged character",
take your pick.
We need to be tested
to see what we are made of.

The heroes of the past
strove for something outside of themselves,
not found in the shallow waters of home.

No pearl without grit
the Stoics tell us,
no strength without resistance,
courage without fear,
certainty without uncertainty.

Mankind is so amazing
but we are inclined to nod off,
sleep at the wheel
when waters are quiet,
the horizon untroubled.

Some lucky few follow their star
but for most, we are quickest
when the house is on fire,
the boat needs bailing,
discovering ourselves under pressure.

I am the bringer of glad tidings !
We now live in difficult times,
more aware that we need one another,
which we had slightly ignored before,
more aware of the challenge to rise
less we fail and fall.

The times ahead will require great effort.
How will they find us ?

StealthStrives, 23 August 2022

75.

Words Worth

A child born in China learns Mandarin,
no need for grammar tutorials,
"I, we, you" clearly understood,
along with "now, tomorrow, yesterday."
Clever mind !

We learn what is around us,
50 words for snow if that is useful,
speaking without effort,
thoughts running helter-skelter through our minds
like excited children.

Words, the clever atoms of language,
building blocks of thoughts, ideas,
basis of plans, intentions, laws, commandments,
neutral in themselves but with great power,
to be fought for, followed, resisted.
Peace, Love, War, Tyranny.
Take your pick.

Words have consequences
as anyone who's blurted out a secret knows.
What is said cannot be unsaid.
You may delete a message on your phone
but you can't take the words back,
can't put the genie back in the bottle,
"Least said soonest mended."
Wise (18th century) man !

Words have power
which can be diminished by overuse.
Some experiences should not be retold often
lest they become mere stories.

Shameful secrets however should be told,
or at least written down,
to release the shackles,
set free the prisoner.

Words, made of letters,
or in truth, vibrations.
How clever is that !

If you were deaf from birth,
you'd think in sign language
using the same part of your brain.
At the risk of repeating myself,
clever mind !

"Sticks and stones... but words will never hurt me."
Tho' most of us can forget anything but a slight.
If I had a tattoo, I'd want Eleanor Roosevelt's dictum,
"No one can make you feel inferior without your permission."

Words Worth ...

StealthSpider weaves thoughts with words, 24 August 2022

76.

First the DNA Dance

The DNA discoverers,
Watson, Crick,
presented the Double Helix
as I discovered reading.

An accidental friend,
John Sulston,
also ennobled (2002)
for mapping the genome
of humble earthworm,
Caenorhabditis Elegans.
Elegant indeed.

He fought to give it away,
made all knowledge available
before our wealthy neighbours
could snare, own, patent.
A mighty man,
this our Professor of Punting.

I see another dance,
"In the beginning was the Word,"
which are mighty, powerful words,
but surely presaged by the Thought.
In the beginning was the Thought ?
which sadly lacks same power of poetry.

We think and speak in words,
words, the seamless multicoloured garment
of our expression.

But the being within
that gives it shape and form
is thought, our thoughts.

We say what we think
if we are wise,
but if we are wiser
we watch what we say
as this shapes what we think.
So much of life is beyond our control
but "self-control" in this small thing
is not.

Let me show my workings
(an "old school" concept).
When we are happy, happy thoughts,
when we are sad, sad mindset,
when I am depressed ...
None of us are perfect,
ain't that the truth,
but we see what we look for
so, prudent to look wisely,
leave much unseen.

So I leave you with this image,
Thought and Word in formal dance,
much like our double helix
with Thought gracefully leading.

StealthRemembers Rosalind Franklin, 25 August 2022

77.

Thoughts Thunk

Each of us have seen
huge advances in knowledge.
Man on the moon ?
Old hat.
Describe the atom ?
Easy-peasy.
Map the human genome ?
Been there, done that.

"You Sir, at the back ?"
"A question, please ?
We know the amazing deeds,
frontiers pushed back continuously,
but what of the thoughts
that created them ?"

"What is a thought ?
Where does it come from ?
What indeed is consciousness ?"

The Speaker paused, scatched his head,
but the questioner had already left
knowing there was no answer to his questions
(that the Speaker could give, at any rate).

StealthThoughts (Cafe Misto, Bailgate), 26 August 2022

78.

Normal

Yesterday we stood apart,
held our breath
behind our masks.

Today, an amnesia,
no thought given,
no precautions taken
against the virus that lives amongst us.

How does this happen ?
“Simples !”
The road from abnormal to normal
is fleetingly brief in the mind's eye
which is how we see.

How else could new parents cope ?
Sadly, not all good news.
We live with situations
which are intolerable:
Antimicrobial Resistance,
Climate Change,
my untidy study.

All quickly becomes normal
to our cost.
Mankind cannot bear very much reality.

StealthLikes Cafe Mistro coffee, Bailgate, 26 August 2022

79.

Perchance to Dream

We control so little
in our lives,
not even sleep.
Sleep comes to us,
a blessing of regeneration,
both physical and mental.

But have a bad night,
tossing, turning,
turning, tossing,
and see who's in charge.

And what of dreams ?
Those chaotic commentaries
receding as you open your eyes.

Nightmares ?
Given that all images
and night dramas
are our own productions,
what do they say ?

Atonia, anyone ?
(That's Sleep Paralysis),
no fun during a nightmare,
I'll tell you !
Learning to relax,
not strain & wriggle,
an achievement
I'm proud of.

If we cannot control sleep,
that's 100 percent true for our unconscious,
where all our memories lie,
all our feelings,
everything about us.

This is a rich mine to work
have we the interest ...

StealthDreams, 27 August 2022

80.

Pavlov's Dogs

We are all
conditioned
in some way.

Act unconsciously
to avoid
past trauma.

After minor
road accident,
I flinch
when cars creep out
from the left.

(Pavlov's Dogs
took longer
to "break")

Growing up,
top floor of house
creaks and shadows
monsters under bed.
Now when alone
at night,
I am "alert",
start at any sound.

Many other stories,
not mine to tell.

Let go too far
and we can't
leave the house.

Courage in life
takes many forms.
Meeting our fears,
doing that which
we naturally avoid,
retaking lost territory.

StealthWalks Pavlov's Dogs (or the other way round !), 12 September 2022

81.

The Timid Iceberg

I know so little
of myself,
have nothing to show
of what I am.

In truth,
the better part of me
lives in dark depths
unknown to me.

What you see
is the lesser
part of me.

I see you
as the same.

StealthSails safe from icebergs (Bay of Biscay),
12 September 2022

82.

Speed of Sight

He walks
and sees
everything.
Or so he thinks.

We are here now
because our ancestors
lived in danger,
stood still or ran,
hid behind bushes
at any unknown sound.

We have not lost this,
especially
on dark streets
walking alone.

We think we see
"openly"
but in truth
our mind selects
what attracts,
or the opposite.

You like cars, say,
so will notice
every model that passes
to the exclusion
of all else.

I like dogs
and step into
a furry doggy world
at every chance.

As a landlord,
I scan
buildings
for loose tiles,
worn windows,
gutters.

Sounds. I react
picking up an Irish lilt,
a Spanish conversation,
engaging instantly.

If the Mind
tugs your coat
to draw attention
to what you like,
it "paws" harder
at what you dislike.

Piercings and tattoos,
body posture,
mismatched colours,
Inner Critic
constantly refreshing
its settings !

So, do you see
what I see ?
Unlikely,
moreover our seeing changes
according to our mood.

It is so easy
to reinforce
what we see,
carving deeper
the ruts
we walk in.
Seeing less.

StealthSees through a glass, darkly, 12 September 2022

83.

A Lesson Learnt

It’s hard to feel cool in a face mask,
to be sure I feel more like a clown,
looking back at the things that annoyed me,
the “small stuff” making me fret and then frown.

But then came some problems of substance,
COVID, the Great Bear picking a fight,
all costs surging like crazy,
and the climate... the future's not bright.

We don't get to choose the time we live in,
or the issues that take over the day,
our sole freedom is how we accept them,
draw a line in the sand, not hide away.

Life has a script for each of us,
which we accept or try to ignore.
These hard times will test our mettle,
it's now or never,
alone and together,
just as in all times before.

StealthWorks, 24 June 2022

To Summarise

25 years ago, I was on a beach in Kovalam, Kerala. The sea was warm and the waves were excitingly strong. Then I was sent sprawling to be dragged back out by the greedy undertow. I staggered up as the next wave broke over me. The shore was unreachable tho' it was only a few yards away. Instinctively I turned round to face the waves now menacing, ok terrifying. I dived into the base of the wave feeling its enormous power as I passed through. Again, again, again now realising my strength was fading. Fortunately the might of the waves subsided and I limped ashore gratefully. It could have easily have been so much worse.

It feels like we have been in shallow tranquil waters but suddenly have been battered by successive "waves" – COVID, Ukraine war, Energy costs, Inflation and the Big Daddy of them all, Climate. We don't feel so secure now.

The Stoics say that we cannot find our mettle without being tested. What will we find in ourselves as we rise to these challenges ?

I hope these poems chime with you in some small way.

Stay safe,

Peter Jackson / StealthWorks

Friends and Family

84.

“Hello, My Name is Peter Boyce”

“Hello my name is Peter Boyce."
“May I have this lady’s choice ?"
And so, a turning point in my life.
For that is how I met my wife.

We were both so young at heart
but we both knew right from the start,
tho’ life can't be just fun and laughter,
we'd be together, happy ever after ...

The Middle
(another few decades to come)

Monday 25 July 1966.
The Royal, Courtown.
Peter 17 years 3 months.
Helen 17 years 1 month 3 weeks.

Written for our Ruby Anniversary.
Wedding vows remade.

23 May 2013

85.

Helen Birthday Card

Fair of body, full of grace,
always with a happy face.

Tho' knees etc are quite crappy,
you, my love, are always happy.

Ammy, Grammy, Ammy, Grammy,
always happiest with your family.

Uncertainties, we have a lot
but I'm so happy with what I've got !

Love always,
(& bed tea)

A PeterPoem, 3 June 2020

86.

Niamh's Birthday

If Niamh is not running up a mountain,
she'll probably be swimming by a fountain
of water so cold,
how would you not "fold" ?

But Niamh's no quitter,
she's the fittest of the litter,
so I say it clear and loud,
she makes both parents very proud!

A PapePoem on Niamh's Birthday, 18 November 2020

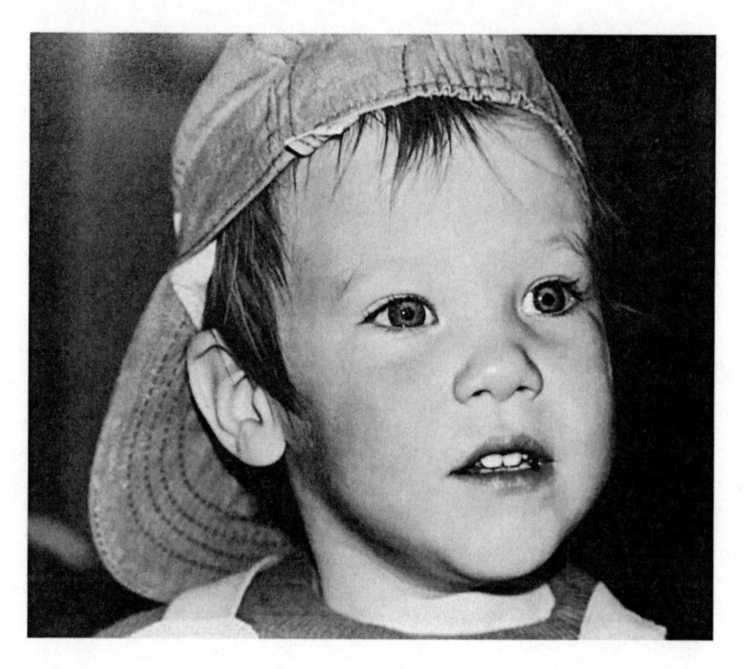

87.

Om

If you're going to have a tattoo,
it had better be blue
and put in a very discreet place.

You don't want to regret
what you did for a bet
and have egg all over your face.

But being an Earth Mother,
Orla cannot do other
than do things with a delicate grace.

"Sound of the Universe" you say,
that's good, any which way.
I guess that puts me right back in my place.

With love for your next 41 years,
thereafter remotely!

A PapePoem on Orla's Birthday, 18 November 2020

88.

"Time Flies By" (for Aoife Age 4)

"Time flies by"
but is it so ?
Let me have a go
to persuade you.

As proud grandfather I see
this beautiful child upon my knee
as she hops, skips, runs, dances,
jumping, handstands, cartwheels, prances.

No sedate walking !
Or considered talking !
But a babble of wild ideas.

A rocket to the moon ?
I'll do that soon.

Once I've put my babies to bed,
telling them what my teacher said.

"Kayley, Don't - You - Start !"

A Pape Poem, 23 April 2020

89.

Born Ready (for Gaia Bear – 3½)

If only I could ask you this question,
find out what I don't understand.
How do you know all will love you ?
How are you so secure in this band ?

When you bellow
♫ TONIGHT IS GOING TO BE A GOOD, GOOD NIGHT ♫,
singing tunelessly with all of your heart,
where's the doubt that afflicts other people ?
You've been so lucky never learning this part.

How do you know you're accepted ?
Smiling up from this lap then that.
Looking up to your sister and her friends.
Always assuming you're part of that pack.

I retract my ridiculous question.

You are what you are.
A very bright star.
We're all blessed to share in your light.

StealthWorks on 31 March 2022

90.

Milo, Good Luck on Starting School

For Milo, our precious boy,
who brings us so much fun and joy.
How exciting, your first time at School
with your own desk and your own stool.

You must wear clothes, that'll be a start,
and when Teacher's close, don't burp or fart !
Speak loud and clear, that's always good,
then home for supper and some pud.

Poor Sophie will miss you when you're away,
she'll be so excited to hear all about your day !

Much Love,
Boppa.

A PapePoem for Milo, 30 August 2020

91.

For Sophie on Day 732

I know a little girl
who had a little curl
right in the middle of her forehead ...

No, No ... No, that won't do ...

So ...

Today, today,
let's run out to play.

But no point saying "Boo !"
Sophie's not afraid of you!
Now that she's Two !

A Pape Poem (Sophie's 2nd birthday), 25 September 2020

92.

Anabella Dawn's Birthday

Anabella's middle name is Dawn,
the name chosen as it was the morn,
after the war in the East was won,
five long years, but at last it was done.

Dad, Greenes, so many relatives took part
and it must have taken considerable heart.
Since then, Seventy Five years have passed
and we hope and pray it will be the last.

Amen.

A PeterPoem on his sister's birthday, 16 August 2020

93.

Welcome To Rossa !

Welcome to Rossa !
You must think you're the Boss-a.

(If your parents cared one little bit for aspiring poets, they'd have called you 'Ross', but 'like the Murphys, I'm not bitter')

For every time that you cry.
your parents just fly ...
"Is his nappy wet or dry ?"
The way that you lie ?

"Has he had a BM ?
Christ, it's only 3 am !
Does he need milk ?
Does he have wind ?
Good God, it could have been twins !"

Rossa, Rossa,
Enjoy being Boss-a.

(It won't last, they'll get sense)

A Pape Poem (Lincoln Lockdown) 14 September 2020

94.

A Feline Farewell

In Memorium Lilly - 8 June 2020

I can see you sitting there,
normally without a care,
but now much sadness in your heart
as we are pulled so far apart.

But I have it on good authority
that loved cats live on in purr - pet – uity.
Who else to greet owners at top of the stair ?
So, I will be there,
yes, I will be there! ...

To be confirmed ...

StealthLoves cats, 8 June 2020

95.

Andy the "Spotta"

Our friend Andy is a "Spotta",
of mighty planes, he's seen a "lotta".
Every day he looks and looks
and, come the evening,
he writes large books.

He loves his cat,
no doubting that,
and the odd beer, trés bon,
First, Third, Fifth and so on ...

He has his views
on all the news
and he doesn't smoke.
He's just a Top Bloke !

Envelope:
We know how old you are ...
(Surely: "We know where you live" – Ed)

StealthWishes Andy Happy Birthday, 22 August 2020

96.

The Caistor Drive Drive

Christmas looms; I'm not a fan.
If up to me, there'd be a ban.
In fact, this year a different one
without a daughter or a son.

Since March, a hard time for us all,
nothing like it we can recall
but many others with much less.
Hard to imagine the awful stress
of not having enough food
to feed themselves and their brood.

Can we help ?
Can we ?
Cans ...

Collecting Cans etc for Lincoln Food Bank.

MODGA 2020 (Make Our Drive Great Again) (Ha!)

StealthWorks, 28 November 2020

97.

My Friend Les

My friend Les is a medium,
well, that should beat the tedium
of being stuck on the carousel of your mind.
I've lived there and know, that's such a bind.

It's like living in a room with mouldy wallpaper,
edges peeling down; oh to have a scraper
to tear it all down and start anew.
But in this game where we're under review,
who made the mess in the first place ?
And sad to say I can just see my face.

That's where we start
but we don't have to lose heart ...
If we want to awake,
there's some effort to make ...
Help is at hand if we try,
help will come bye and bye ...

My friend Les is a medium ...

StealthWorks, 21 April 2020

Poems B.C. (Before COVID – 2017)

98.

Pedigree

There is pedigree in my past
but little in my present.

But what do I know ?
The truth of stories told
or what I was meant to hear ?

And how can I judge myself ?
Or what I have achieved ?
Always easy to find fault,
especially when faults have multiplied,
fed off each other,
divided,
lain dormant.

What I do know
is that we are all Travellers,
not all equal,
or even at the same stage of our journeys.
The weather has its whims
and the planks and varnish
have their own scripts.
But I can journey well,
hold the sail firm against the wind,
tack and tack again if all else fails
and encourage my fellow travellers
in their travails.

What can I do ?
What can I give ?
A nod,
a glance,
a recognition across the waters
will suffice.

StealthAttempts to write, influenced by Tim Jackson, 15 July 2017

Father/Son
Expo '67, Montreal

Pavilion "Resources of Man"

"Man's Greatest Resource is Himself"

Origin of the photo is unknown but was definitely taken at the races while my father quizically examined the bookies' odds.

"Man's Greatest Resource is Himself"

99.

Invitation

We are matter, yes ...
chemicals yes ...
All fiendishly, cleverly arranged,
but something else ...

Who is the dark shadow in the background ?
Clicking his fingers patiently,
offering the suspended spinning penny,
the darkened lightbulb ?

Waiting for my pedestrian synapses
to fall in line,
to feel an idea,
as if God Himself had whispered in my ear.

My apologies, dear reader,
the mention of God unnecessary exaggeration
but surely, surely, surely,
the quiet voice that speaks means something.

Transmission can be so hard,
there is so much static on the line,
three meals a day & wine besides,
24-hour television ...
Only my Muslim friends fast regularly ...

StealthWorks, 1 August 2017

100.

Moses

The desert is a big place,
no shame in getting lost,
though 40 years... ?
Little food or water, sleep,
only voices for comfort.

Was it fear of being wrong
that drove him up the mountain ?
And then the furious hammering began
which made slaves and worse of us all.

If this had to be,
if this **had** to be,
why not one instruction ?

Each man must find his own mountain ...

StealthWorks, 10 August 2017

101.

Confession

Victoria Tube Station,
so big, noisy, confusing,
"I'm looking for the Coach Station ..."

Two voices came, both correct,
first man casting off quickly,
caught in the London tide.
Behind him remained a tall man,
his face, a picture of past pain and loss.

"Buy a Big Issue, Sir ?"
I hurried on my way,
part London disease,
part meanness on my part.

Instant realisation and regret
but the cock crowed lazily,
enjoying his moment.

As someone who claims to search,
failing to see what is before me,
beyond my comfort zone,
is not enough.

StealthWorks, 16 August 2017

A CIP catalogue record for this title is available from the British Library.

ISBN 9781398493919 (Paperback)
ISBN 9781398493926 (ePub e-book)

www.austinmacauley.com

First Published 2023
Austin Macauley Publishers Ltd®
1 Canada Square
Canary Wharf
London
E145AA